AF255883

RAINDROPS

ARE FALLING ON MY HEAD

JANE BACHE

Published by the Book Incubator 2018
From Storyboard to Print™
www.bookincubator.com.au
Bunbury Western Australia

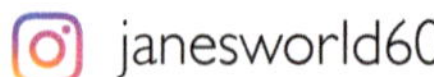 janesworld60

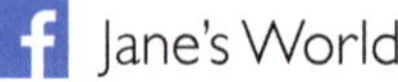 Jane's World

Book layout and design the Book Incubator
Photo credit: Irene Brown pages 22 and 25
Photo credit: Lorraine Eccles page 23
ISBN: 13978-0-6481563-8-3

 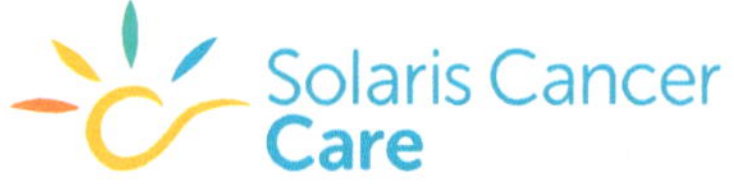

To Barry and Matthias

In life your mateship was infectious.
In death you were brave.

To Blair, Lachlan and Shelby,

I love you to the moon and back.

To Kate,

I am so glad that I met you. Thank you
for helping me to make this book happen.

And to Solaris,

I am and will always be, grateful for your
kindness and support.

Love always,
Jane

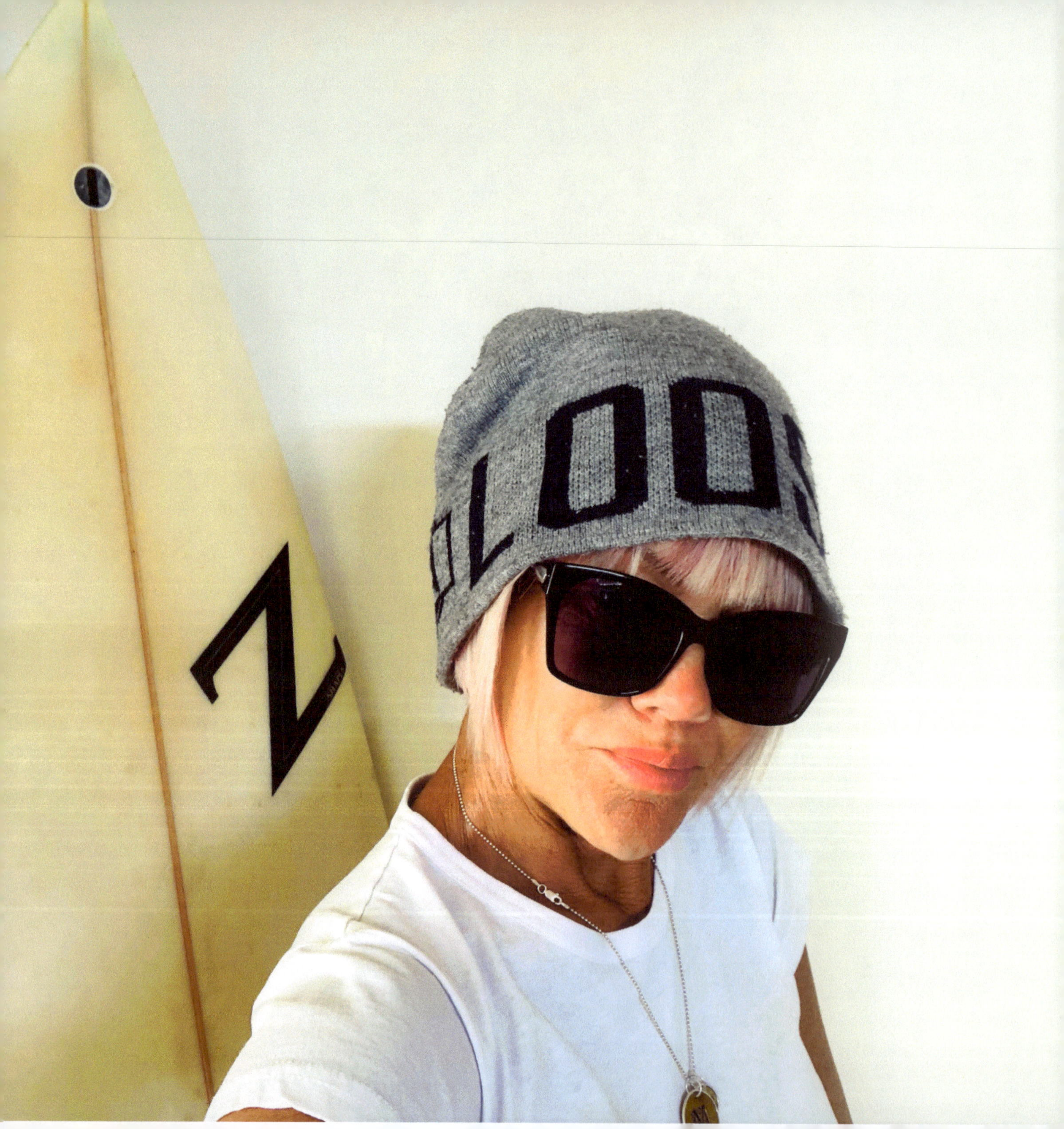

Mother's Day May 11, 2014
I became a widow.
I was 53.

9:36pm March 8, 2016
I got a phone call telling me that my
son was missing at sea.

We never found him.

He was just 25.

Today I am

SASSY, SEXY & ALMOST SIXTY

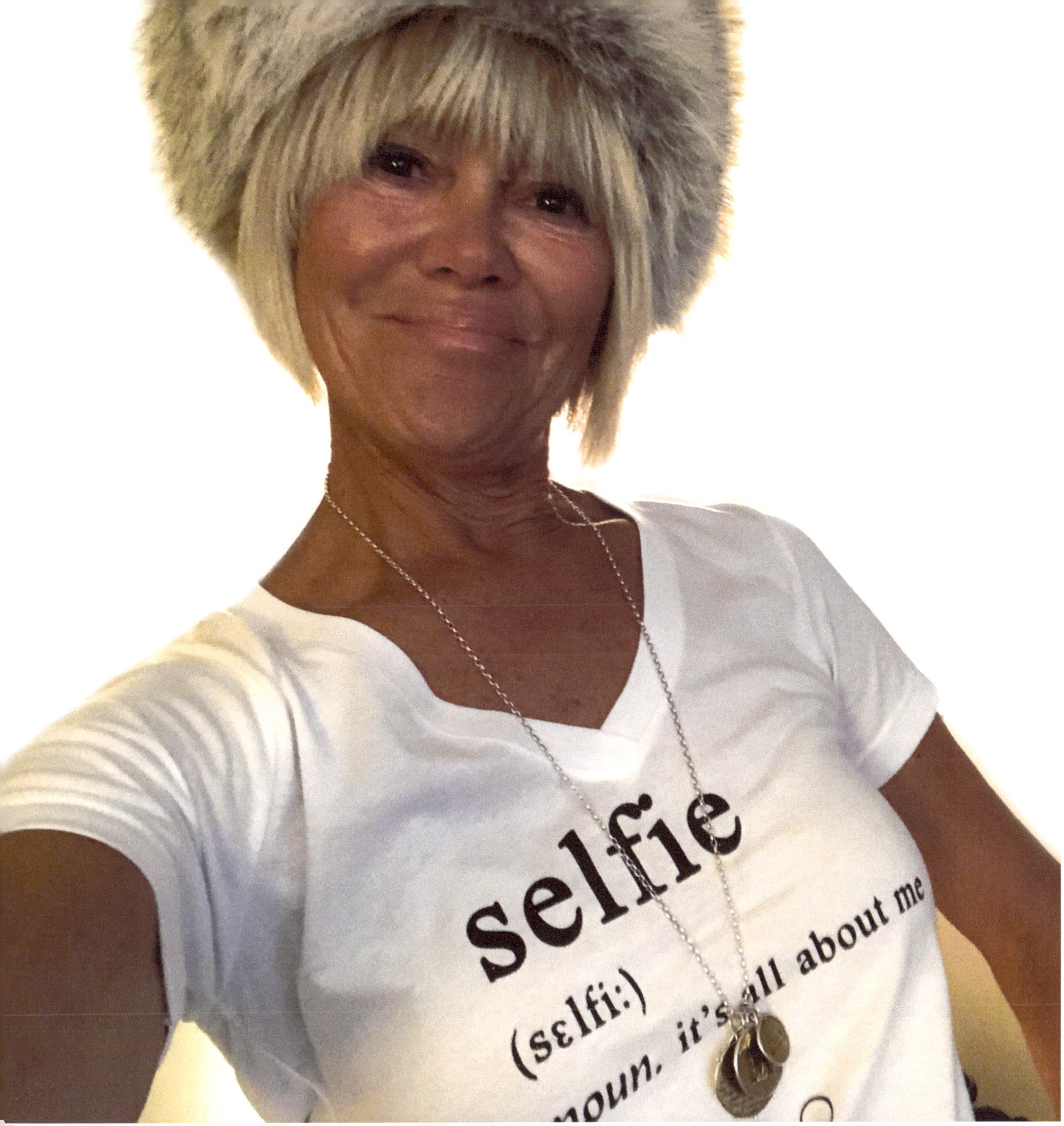

selfie
(selfi:)
noun, it's all about me

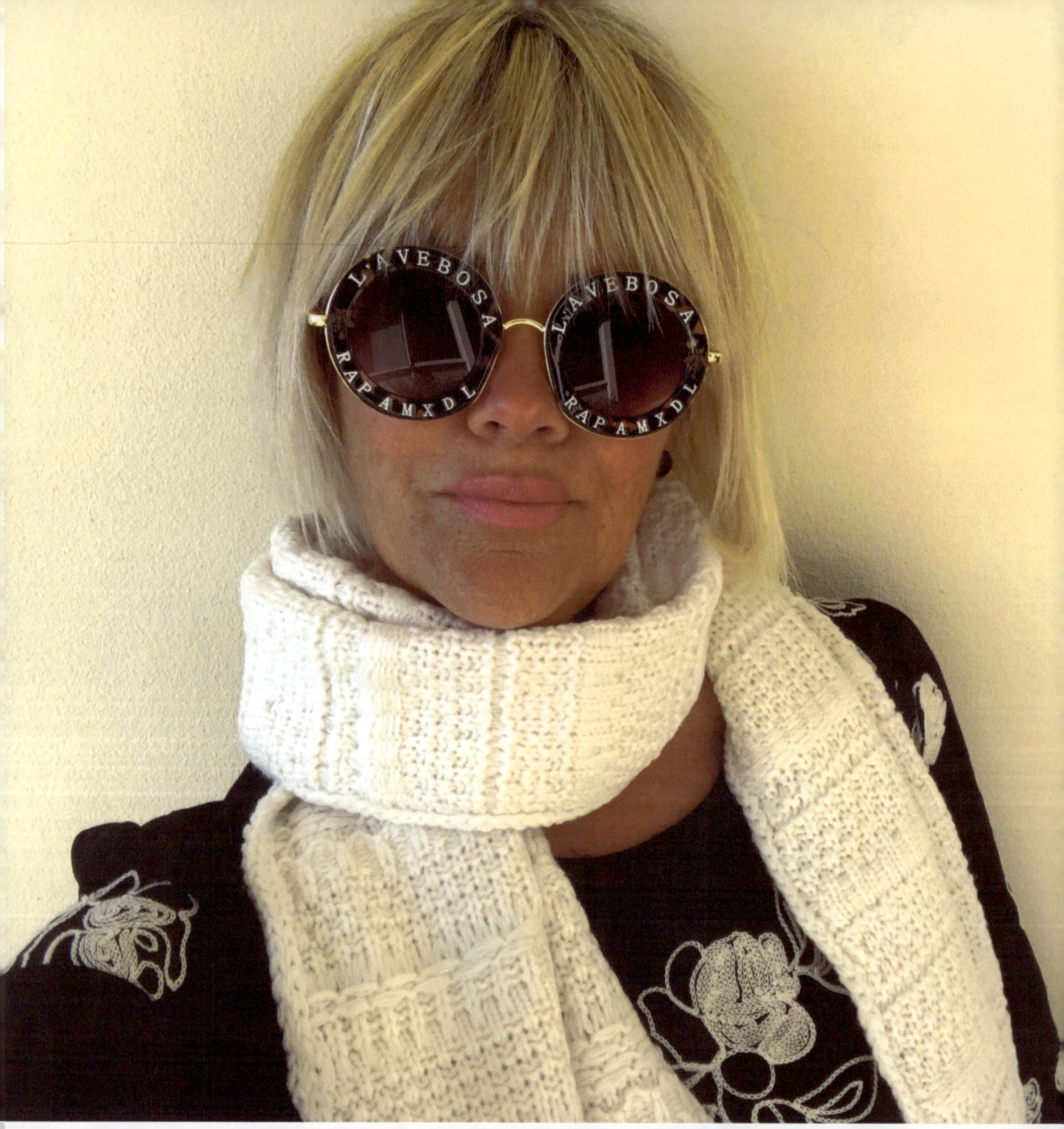
L'AVEBOSA
RAP AMXDL

I made a decision to live my life.

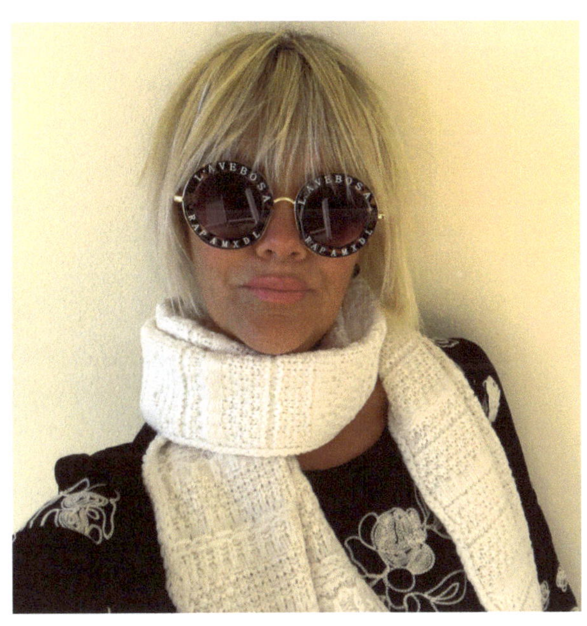

Embrace life

regardless of personal tragedies.

Survive the best way you can ...

Me? I love all things healthy, fashionable, travel &

lots and lots of SELFIES

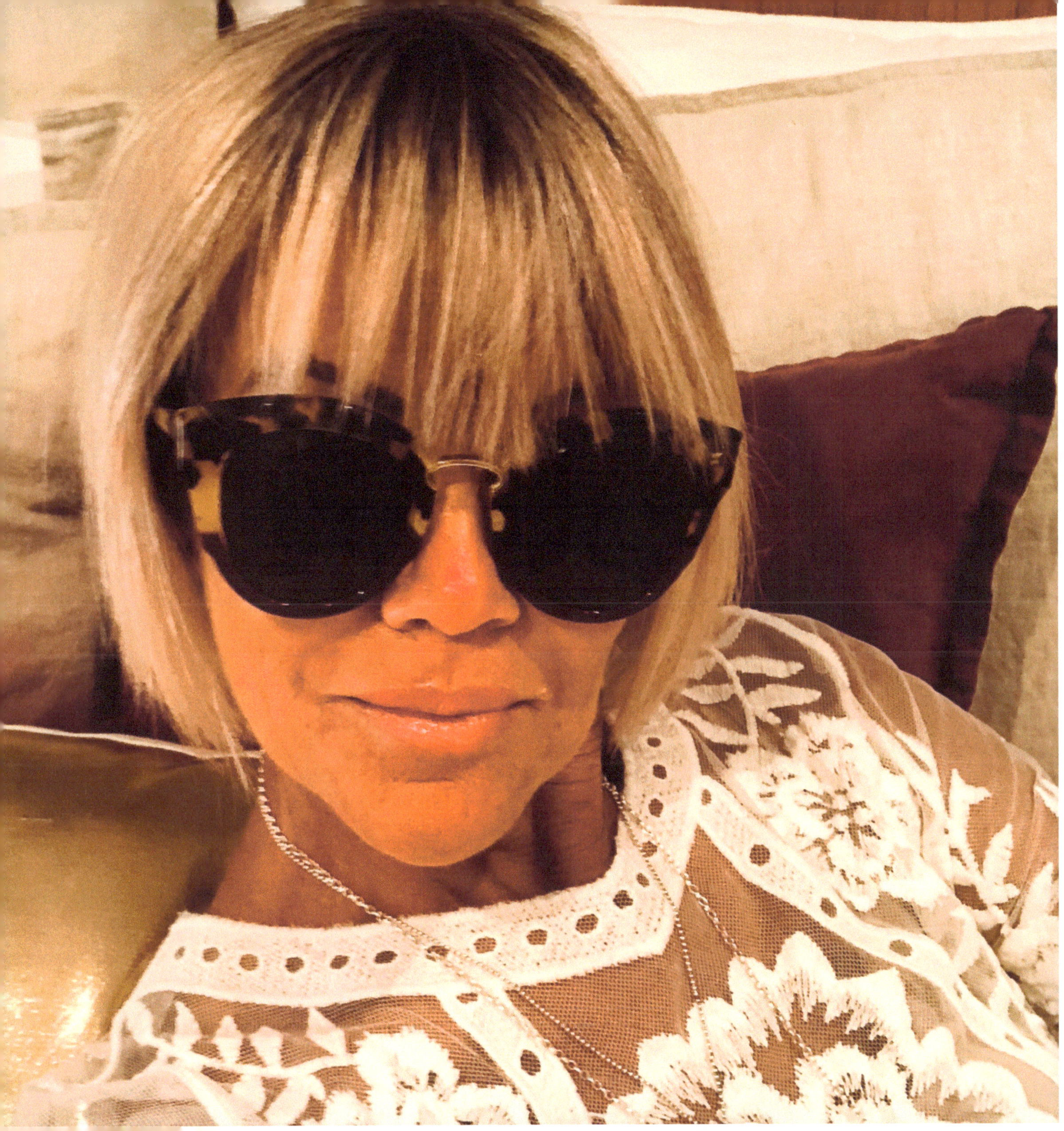

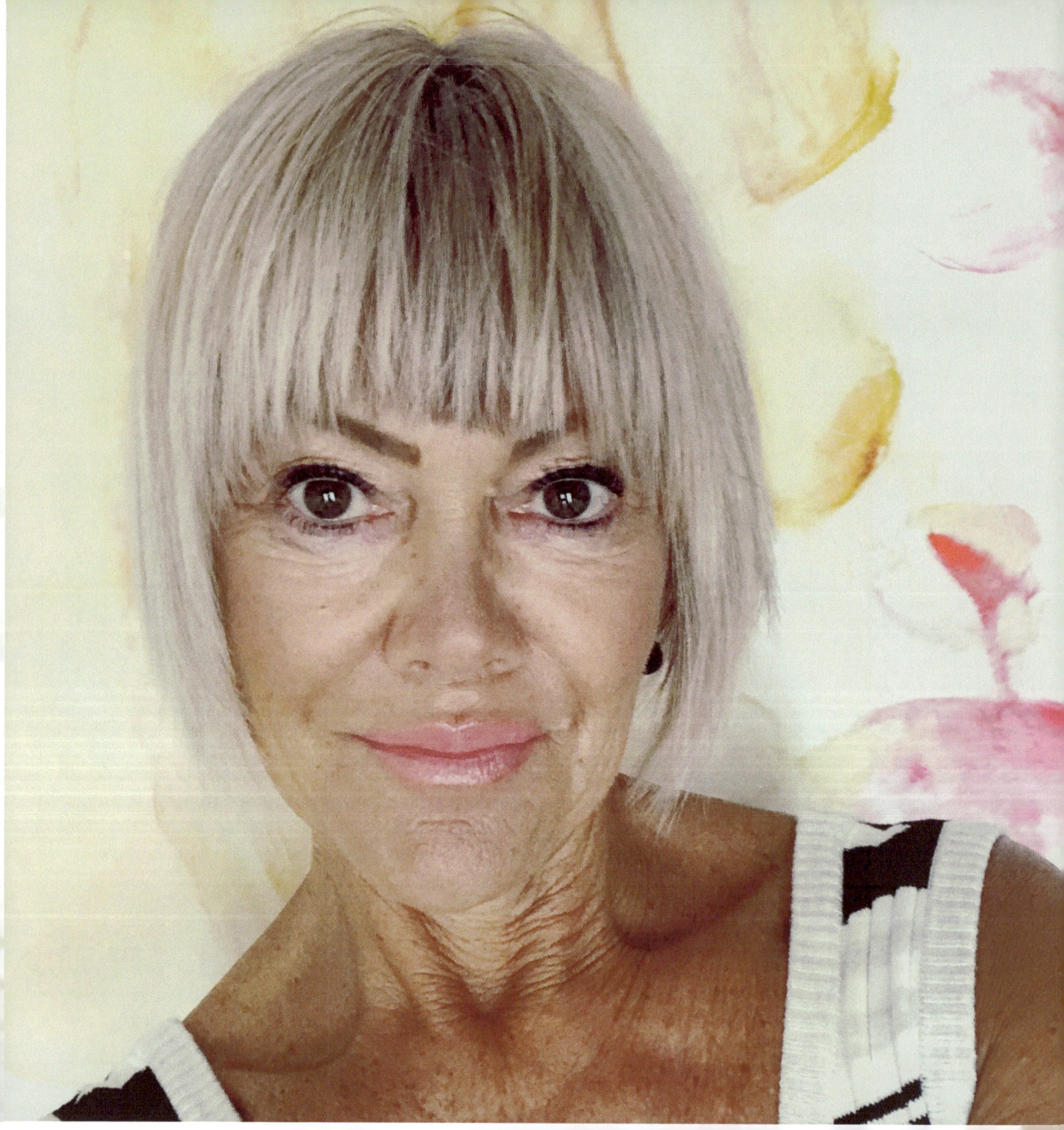

For most of us, first dates usually start with a coffee and a chat.

But me?

I went to New Zealand and didn't look back.

Show up in *every* *single* moment.
Own it!
You are meant to be there!

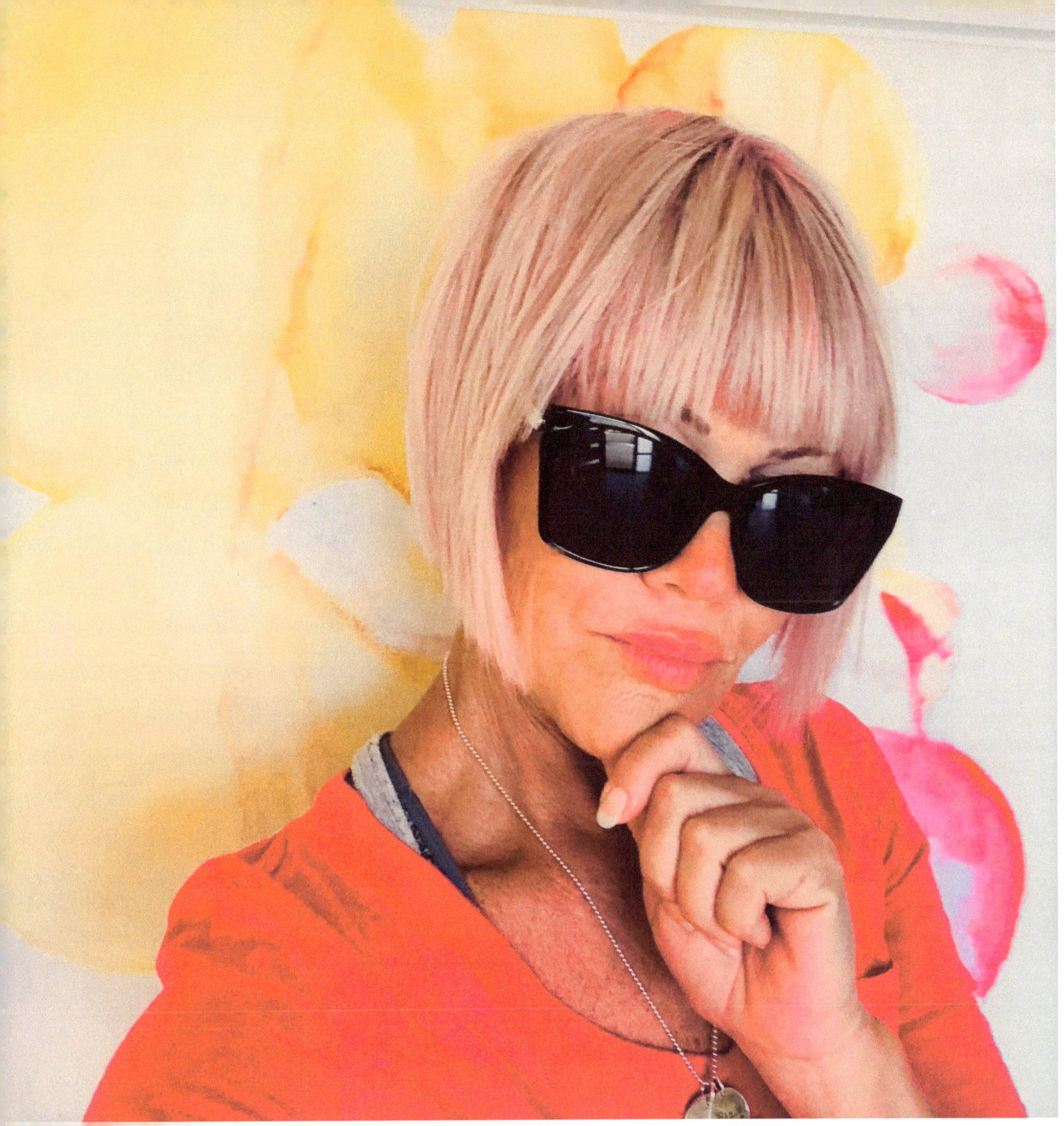

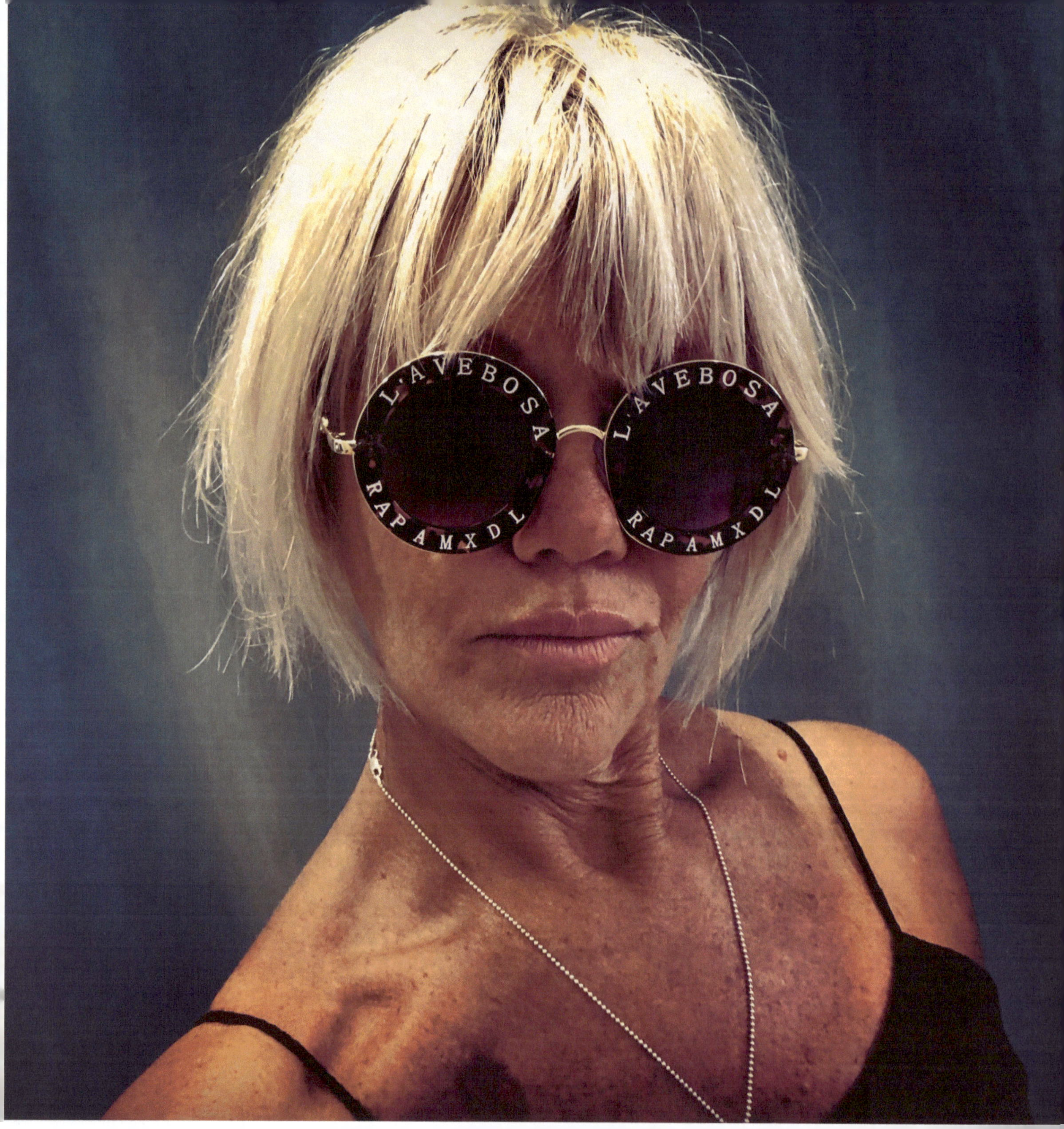
L·AVEBOSA
RAPAMXDL
L·AVEBOSA
RAPAMXDL

Attitude is everything.

Don't mess with me.

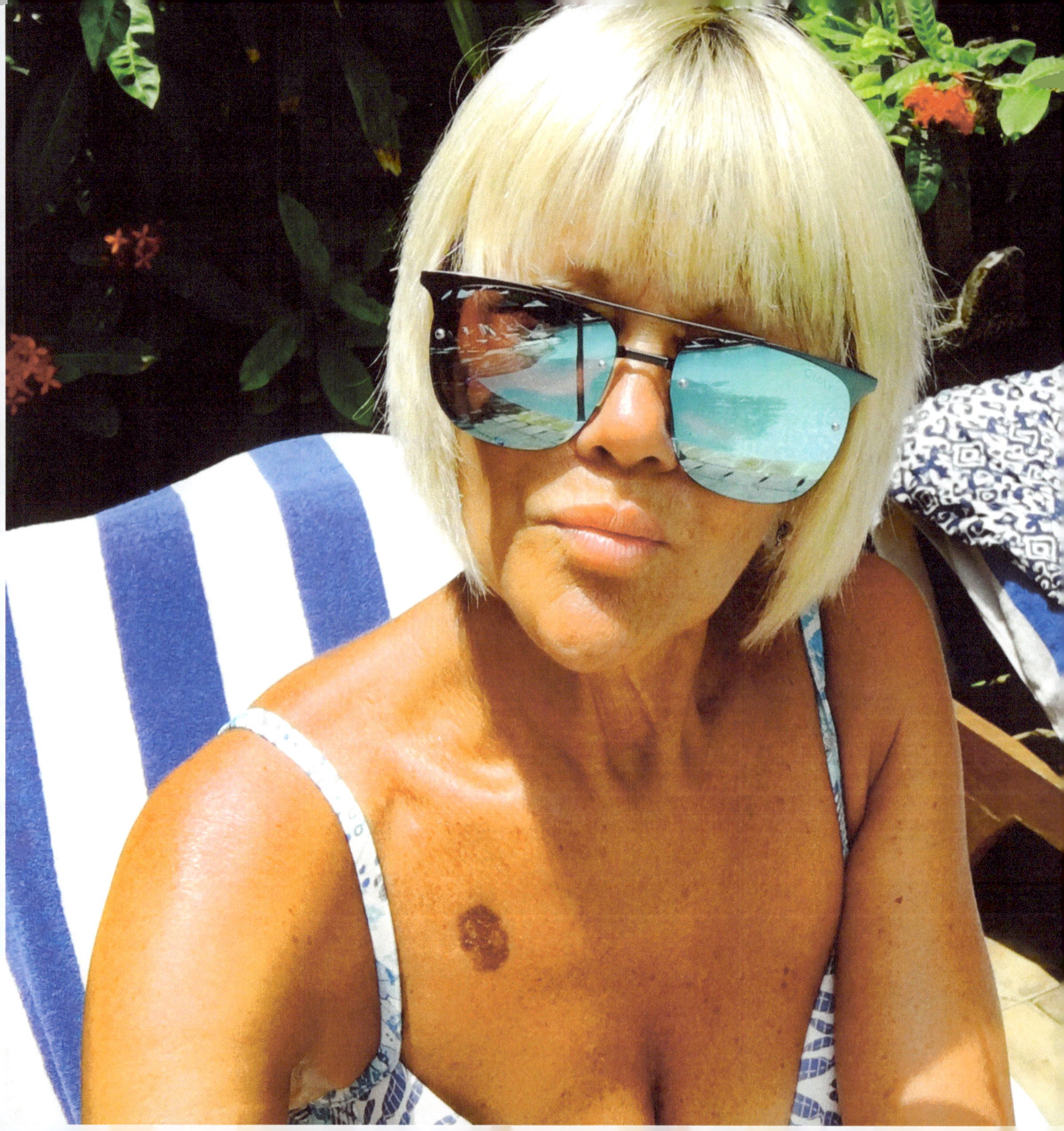

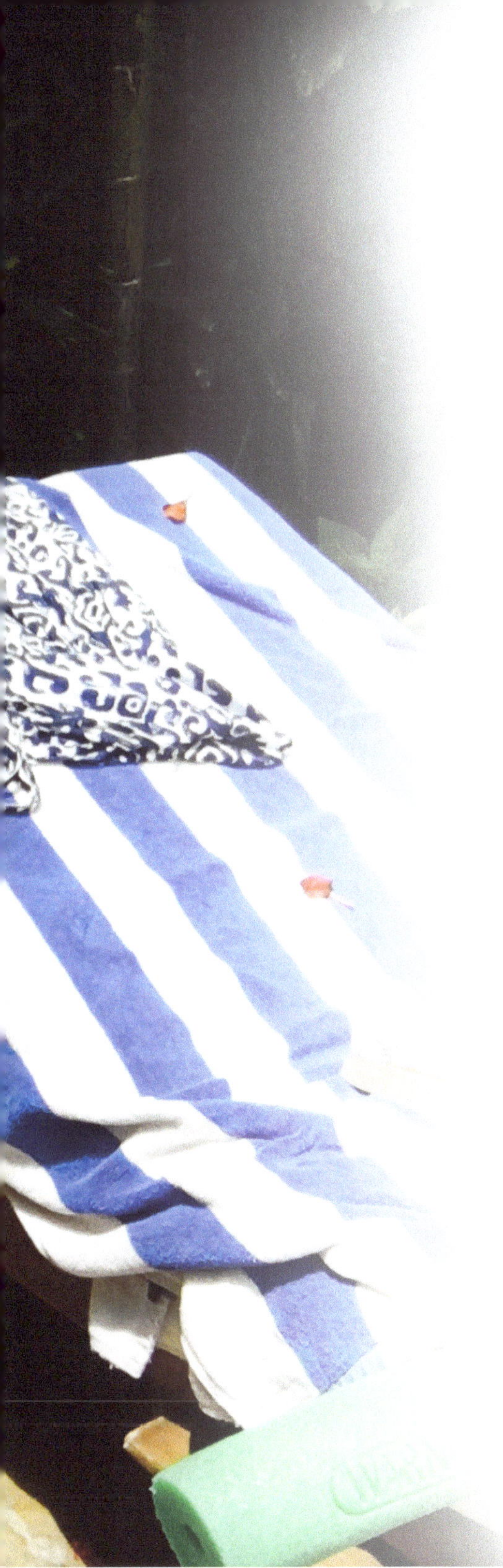

Be kind to yourself.

I went back to where my husband died.
It was hard.
It was nourishing

I can move on.

When you cant find the thing you need ....
Sometimes you need to create it yourself.

Me?

I needed a travel buddy so I joined

Find a Female Cruise or Travel Buddy.

My #1 rules for a travel buddy?

They need to be willing to photograph me!

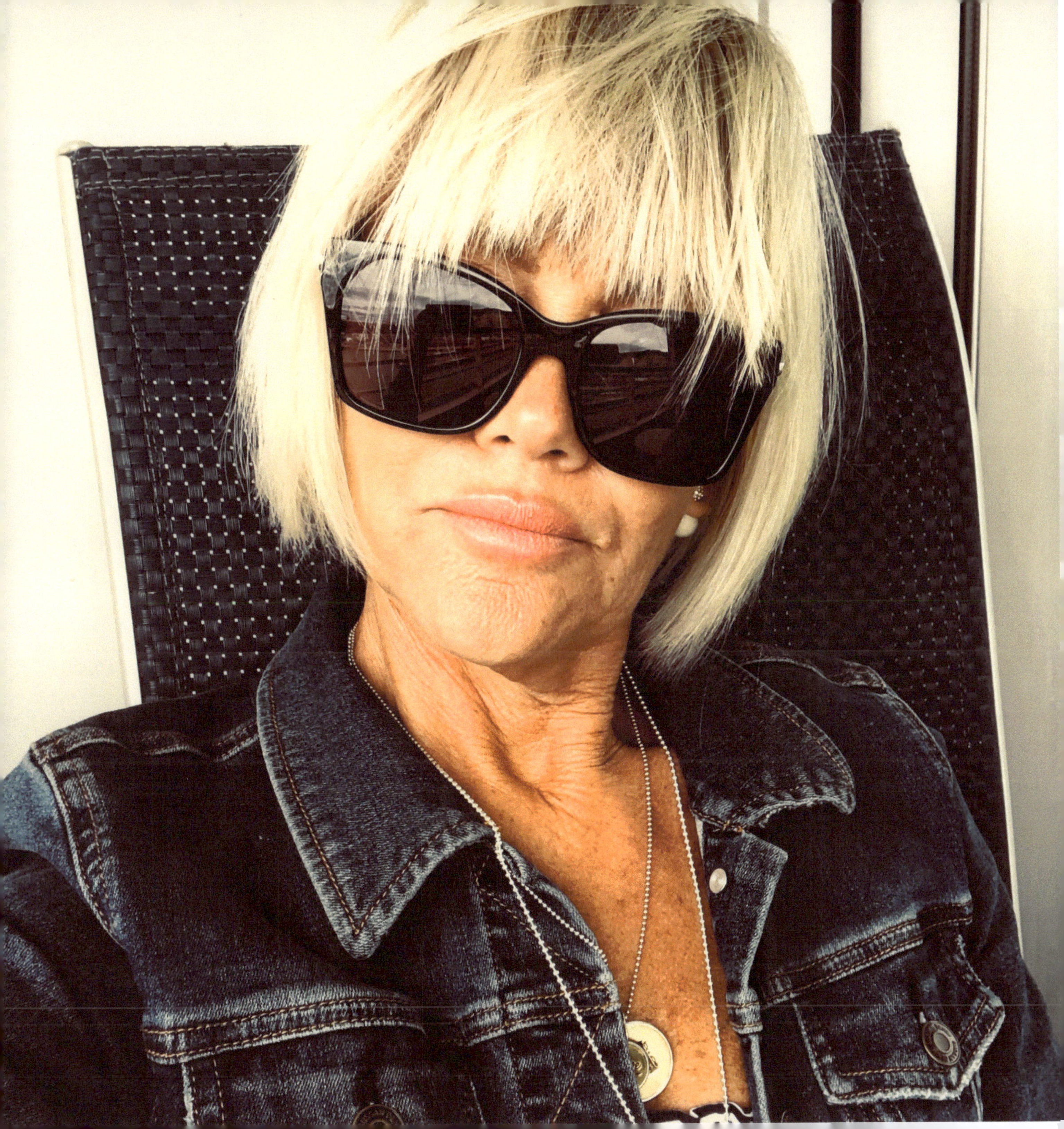

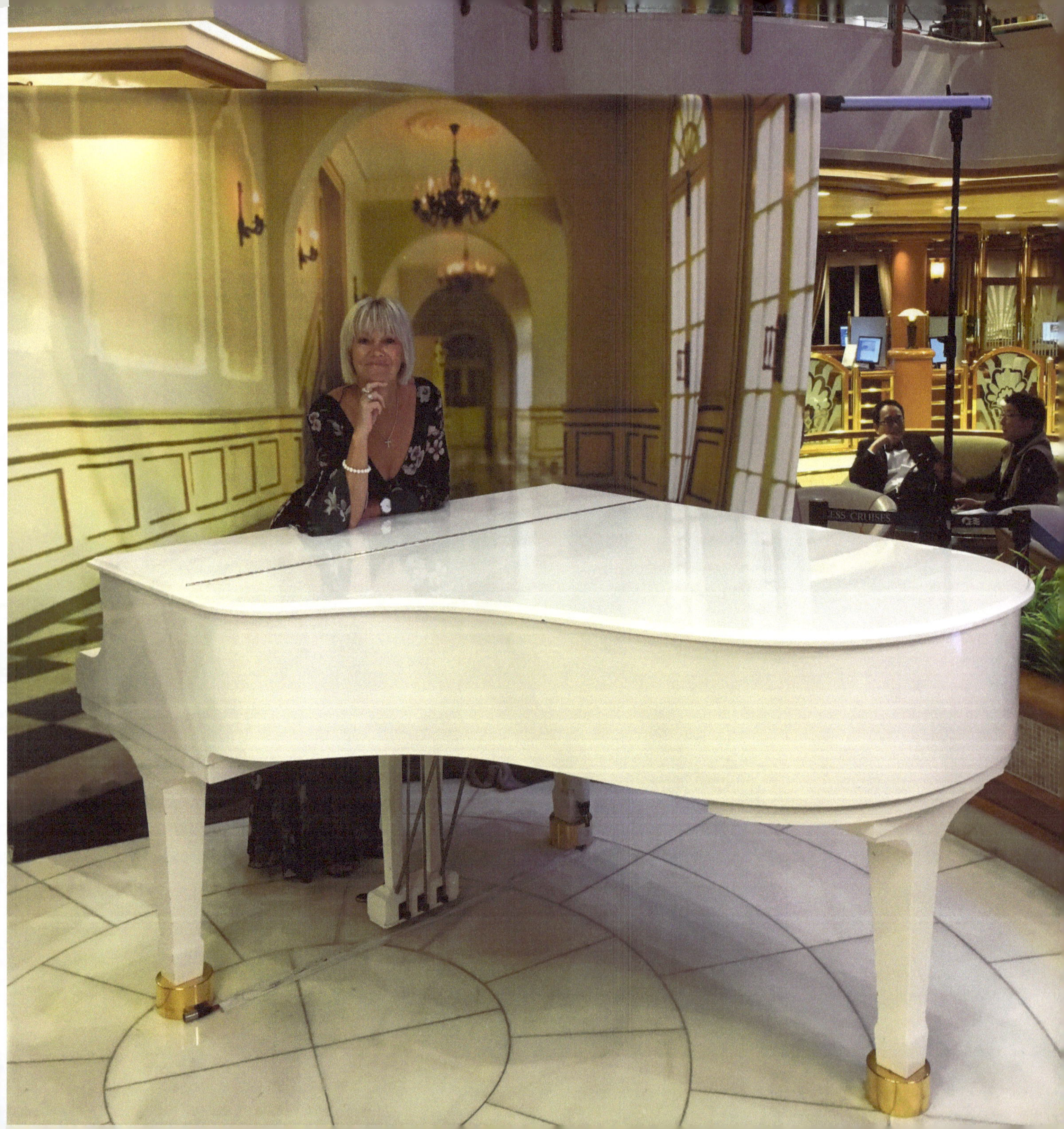

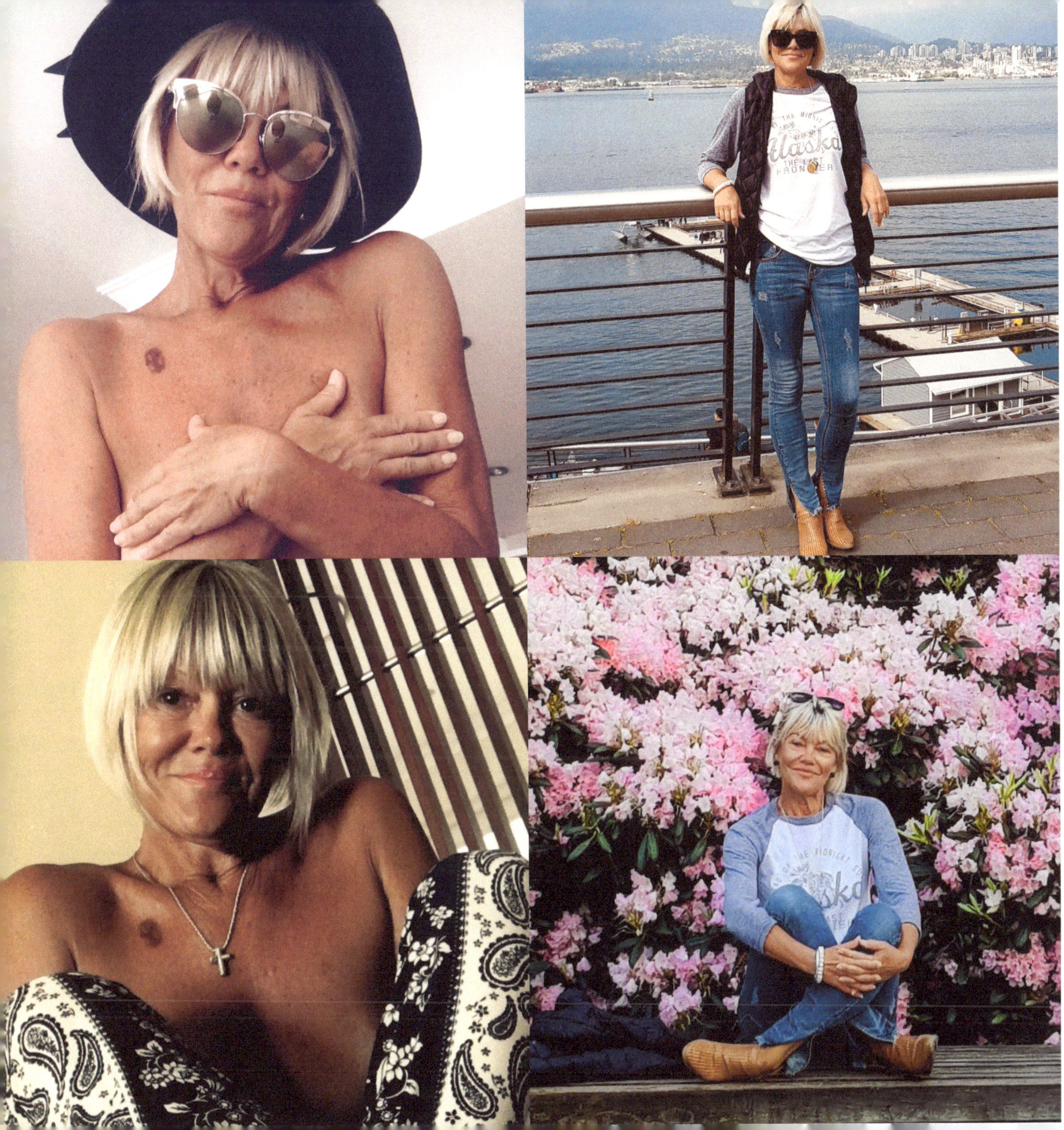

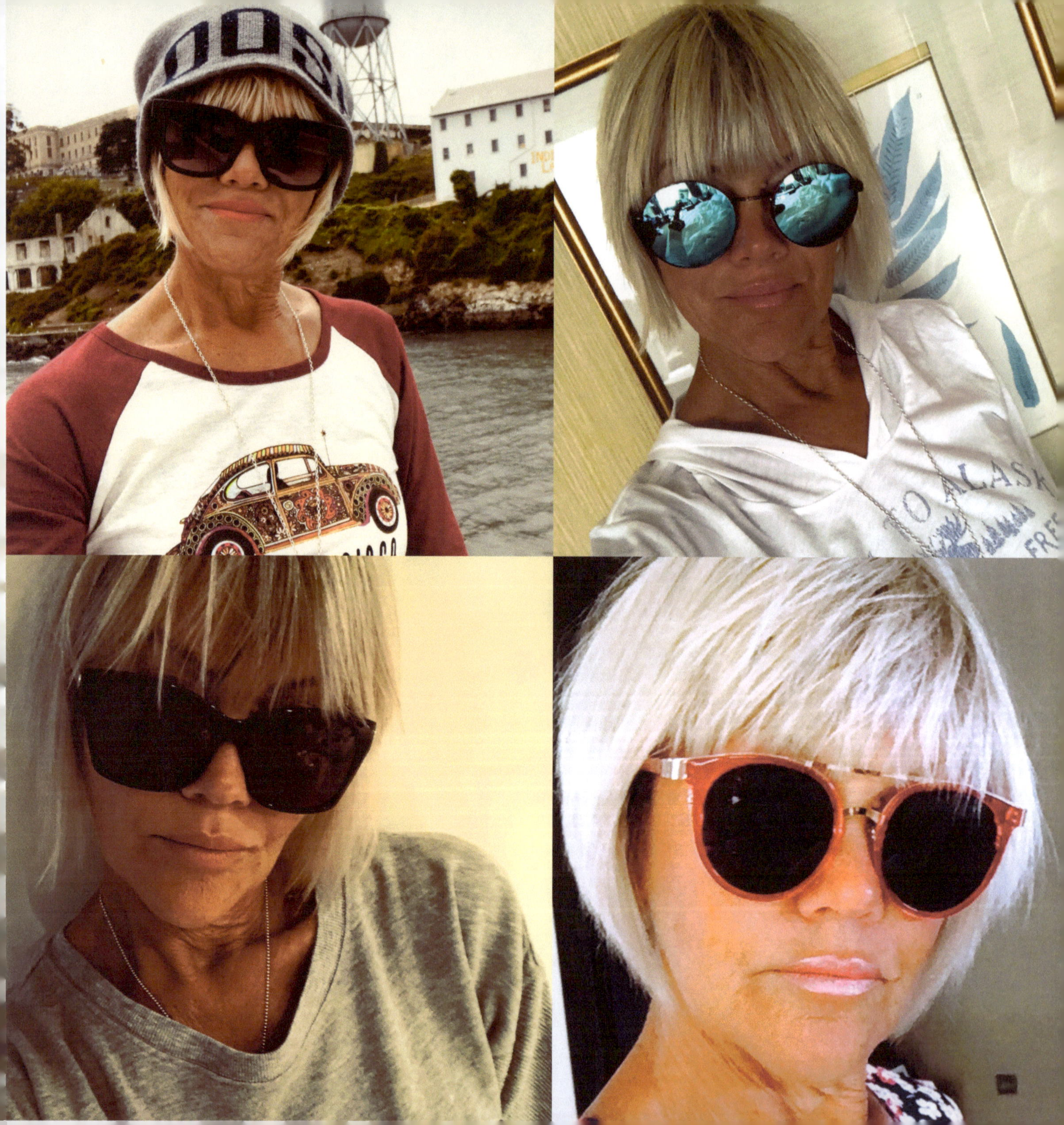

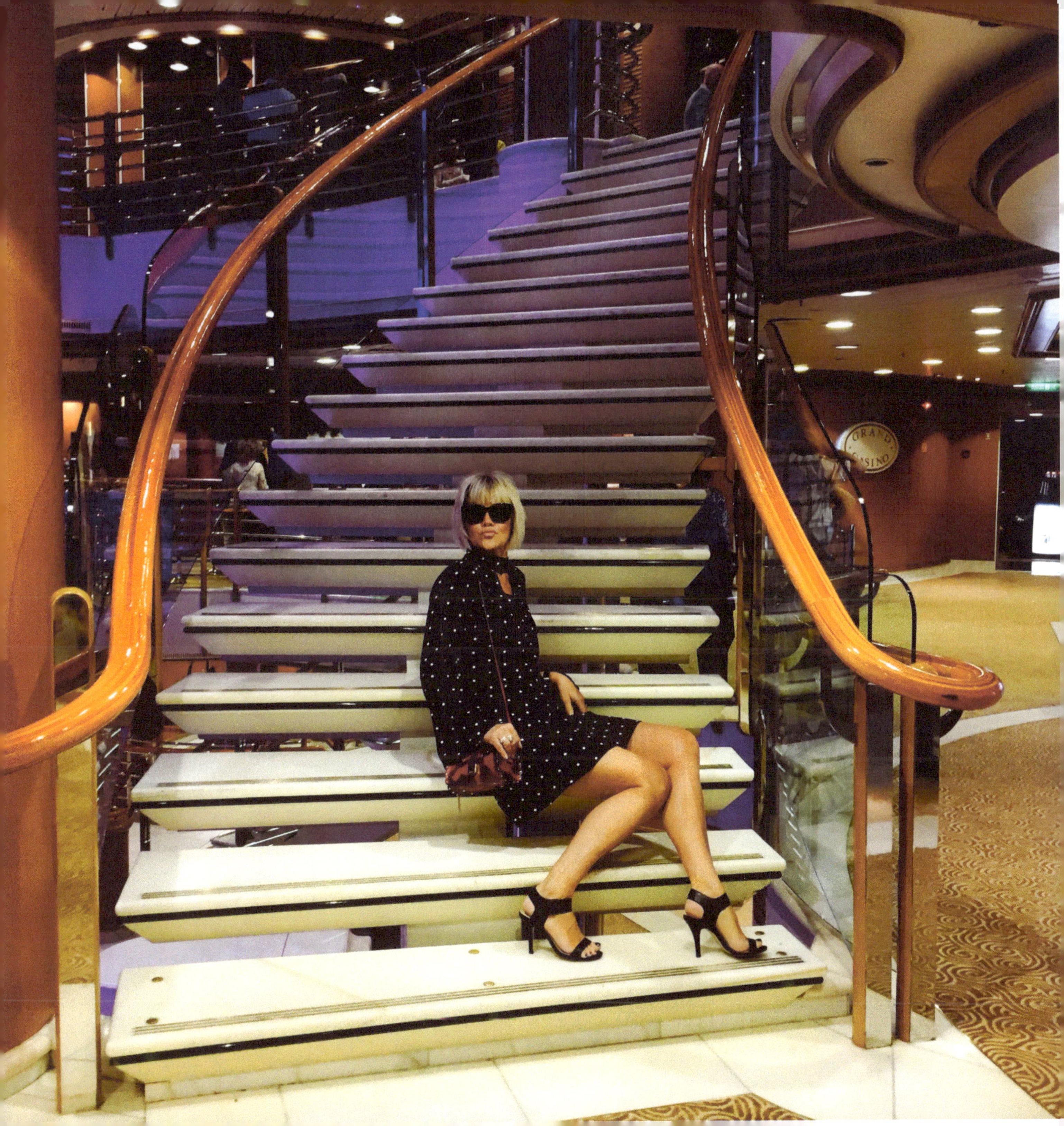

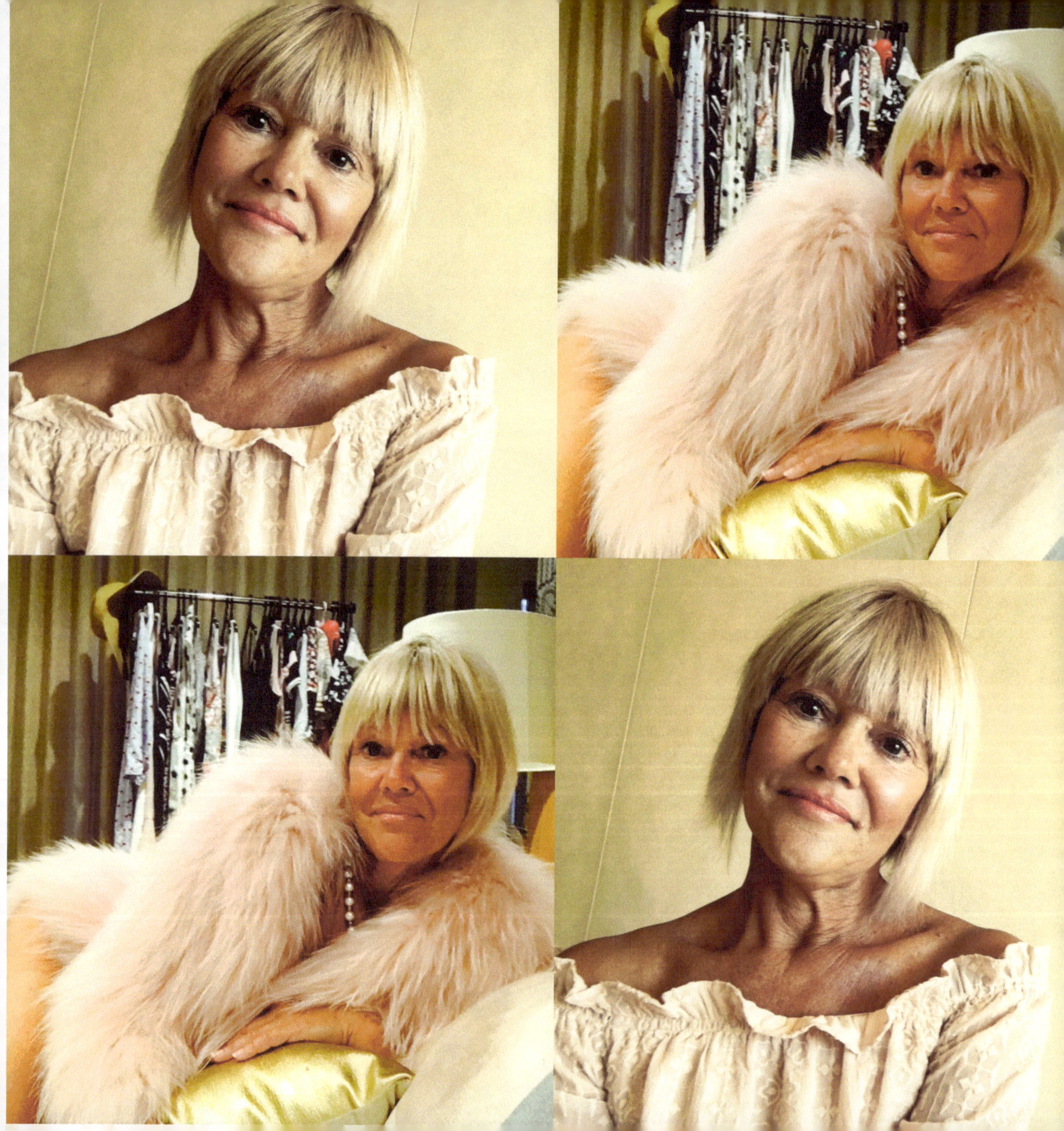

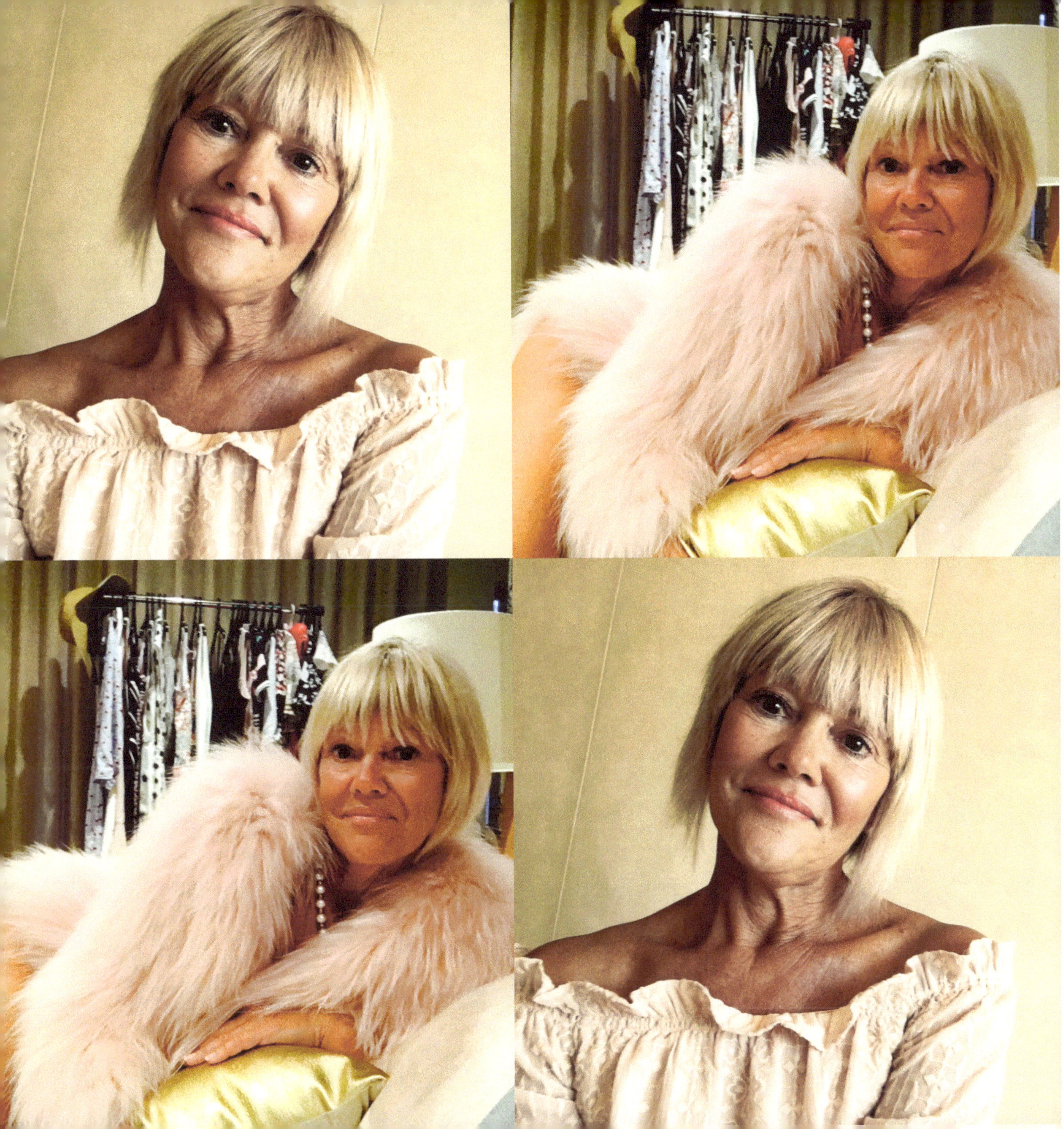

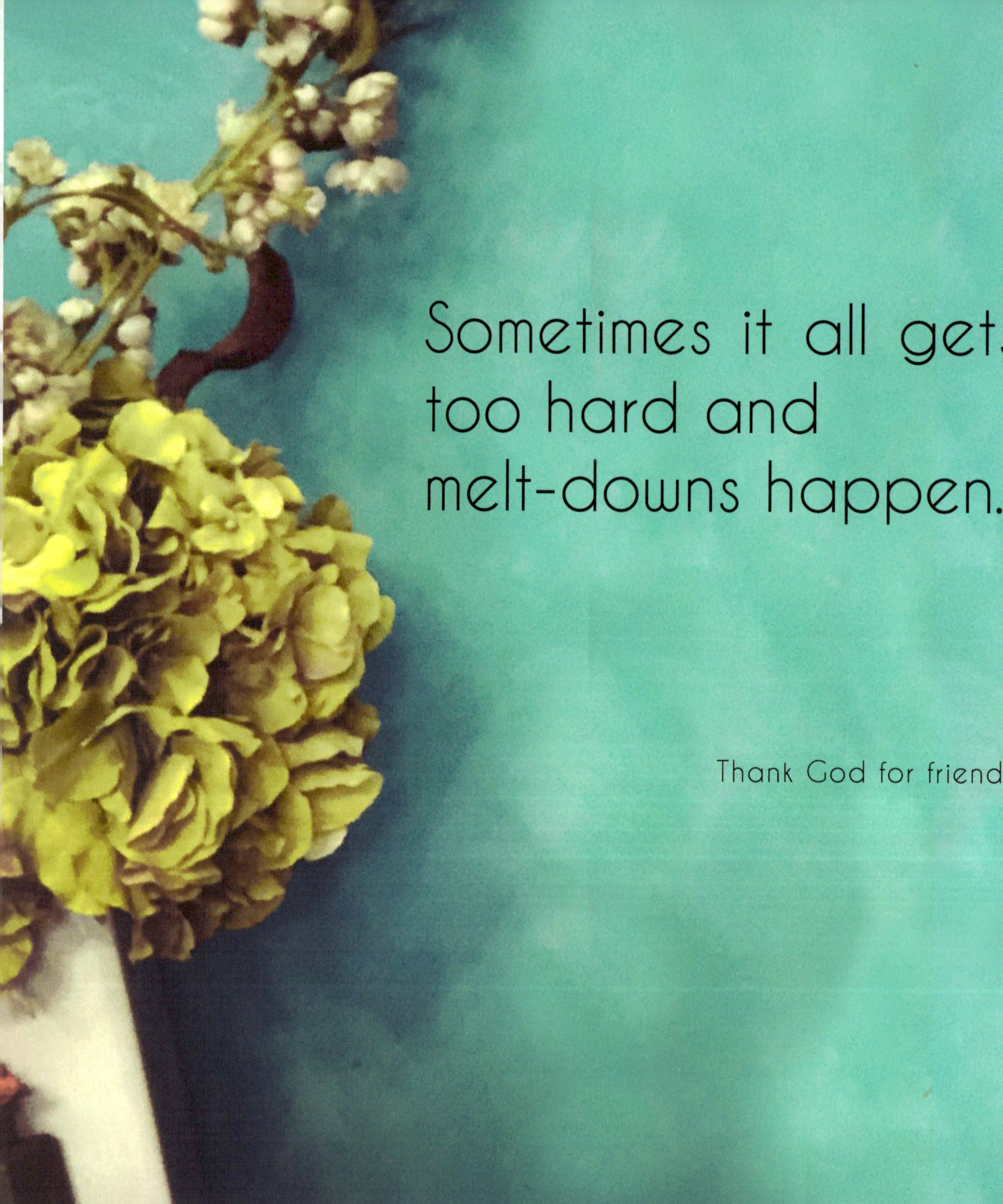

Sometimes it all gets
too hard and
melt-downs happen.

Thank God for friends.

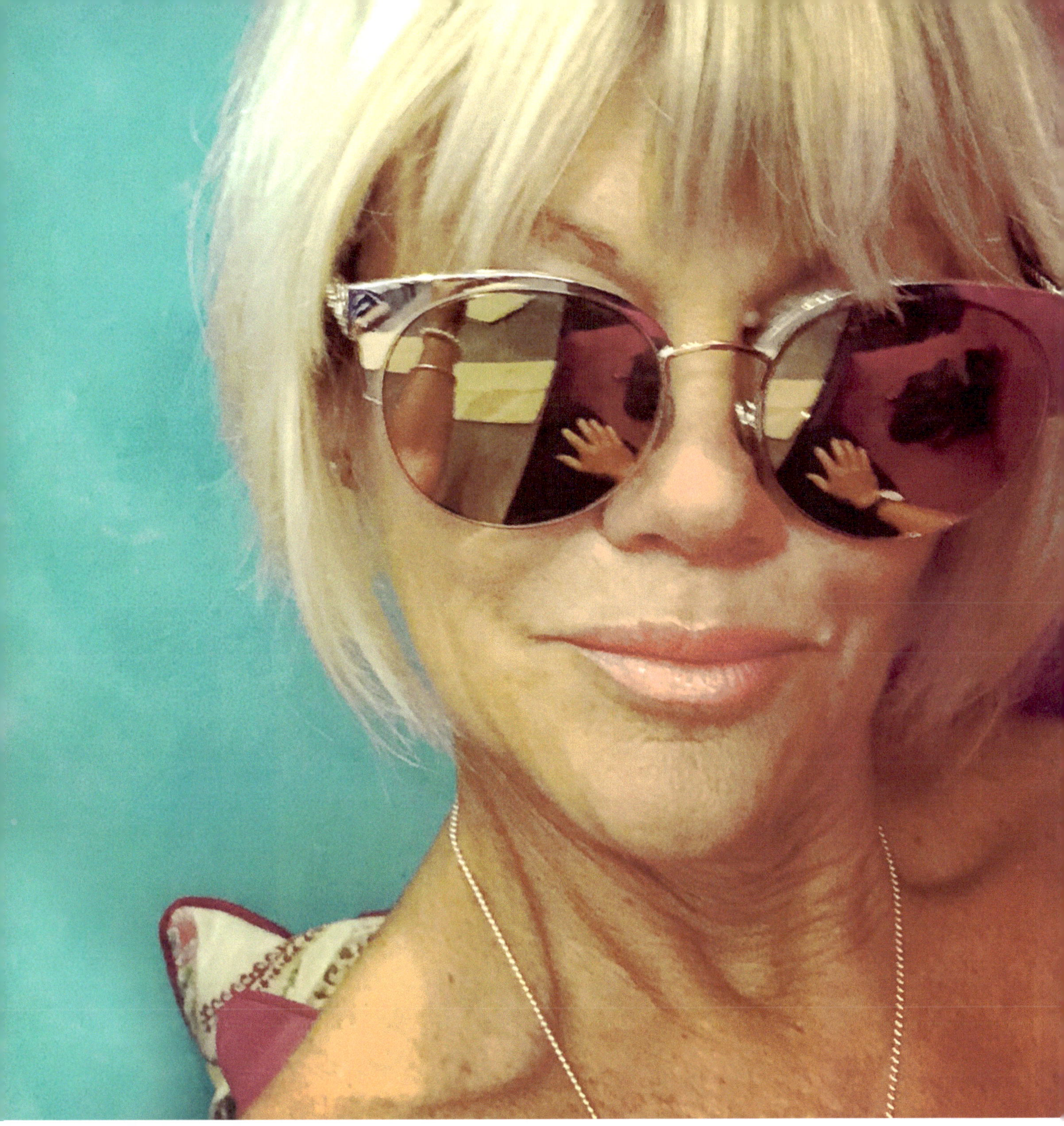

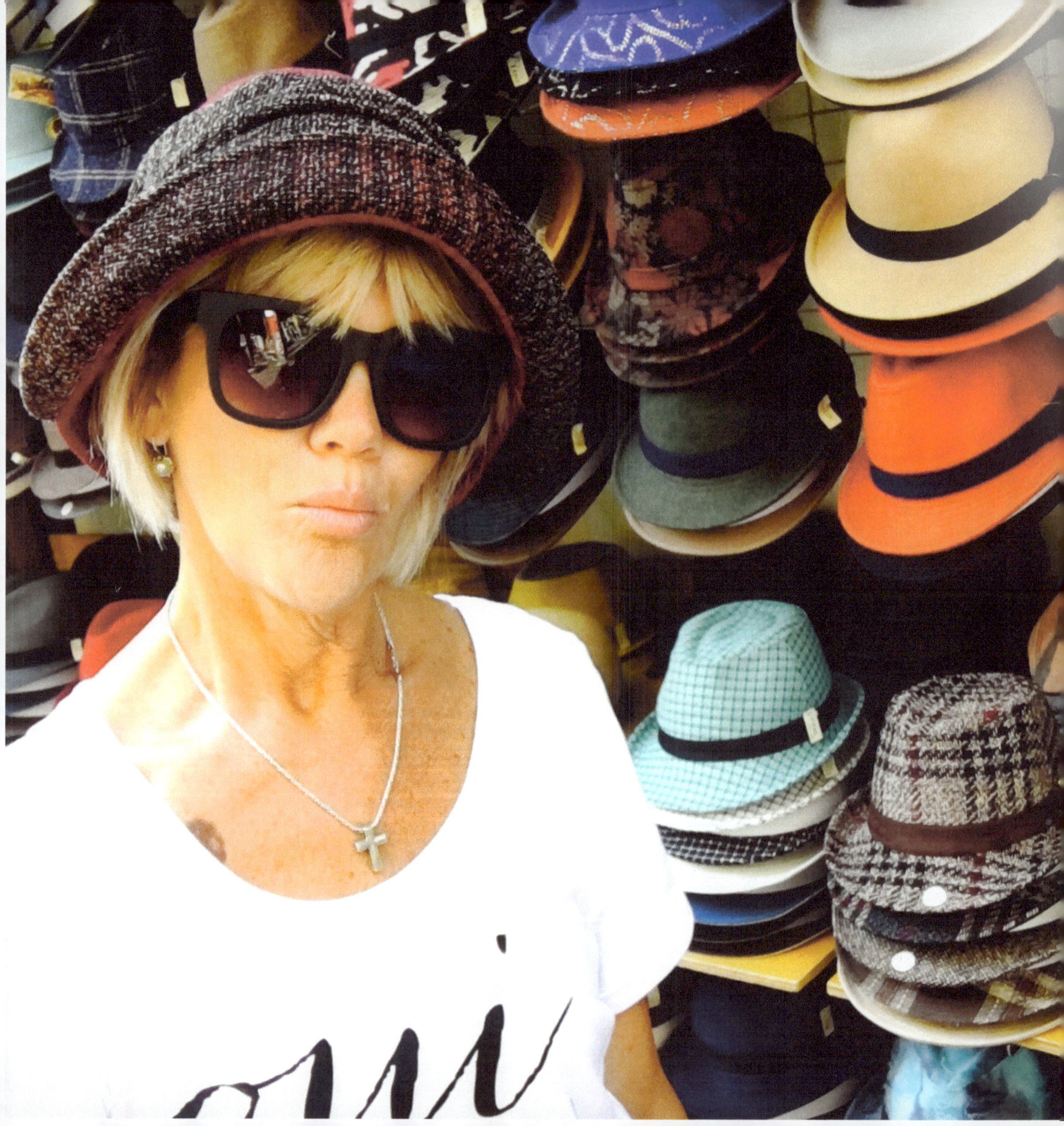

We all wear
many hats.

What hat do you wear?

breathe and

exhale

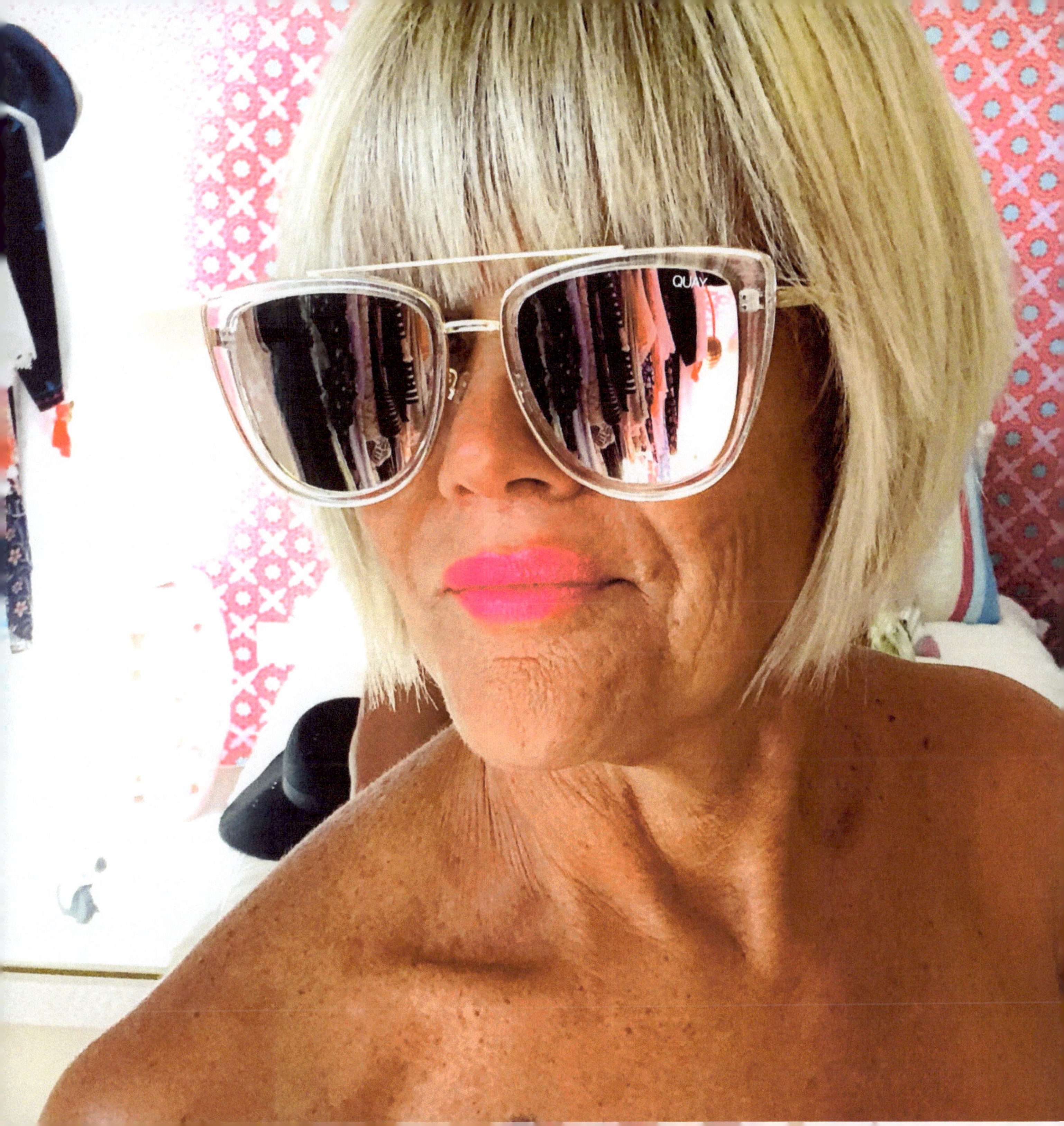

www.ingramcontent.com/pod-product-compliance
Lightning Source LLC
Chambersburg PA
CBHW042203030726
47602CB00007B/105